530 Reasons Why
Deplorables Won

Steve Stranghoener

For Kellyanne Conway, Shaun Spicer, Ann Coulter, Ted Nugent, Clint Eastwood, John F. Kennedy, George Washington, John and Jane Q. Public, you, me and Deplorables throughout history everywhere.

(Yes, in today's world, many of President Kennedy's and other traditional Democrats' views would be considered deplorable.)

Foreword

Regardless of one's political persuasion, 2016 represented an election year like no other. It left pollsters flummoxed and pundits aghast. At the time of this writing, those who voted for the losing ticket remained in a state of denial with some determined to revise history. This book has captured the moment for posterity so that we do not soon forget the reasons behind the popular uprising that brought Donald J. Trump and the Forgotten Man and Woman to power. While purposefully succinct, this book is offered as a serious and, hopefully, thought provoking keepsake. I could think of no better way to get the point across than to pen *530 Reasons* in the blunt, forthright, clipped, Trumpian style that our new president used so effectively on the campaign trail. Please take note that this list is meant to be representative but is certainly not exhaustive. Also please note that, for the most part, these reasons are presented in no particular order. I will leave it to you to ponder each entry and assign importance as you see fit. I've left plenty of room for notes on each page so you can record your thoughts accordingly.

It is not my intention to cast dispersions at anyone mentioned herein. I am simply chronicling people and events that, in my view, had an effect on the outcome of the election. I will leave it to you, the reader, to consider the impact of each citation.

1. Barack Obama

2. "You didn't build that."
3. Apology tour
4. Shovel ready jobs
5. Rush to judgment
6. Cambridge Police "acted stupidly."
7. "If I had a son, he'd look like Trayvon."
8. "They get bitter, they cling to guns or religion."
9. ISIS … "JV team"
10. Leading from behind
11. Iran nuclear deal … pallets of cash
12. Betrayal of Israel at the U. N.
13. "If you like your doctor …"
14. Slowest economic recovery in history
15. $20 trillion deficit
16. Victory laps without victory … premature withdrawals from Iraq and Afghanistan
17. "There has never been any man or woman more qualified for this office than Hillary Clinton."

18. Hillary Clinton

19. Bimbo eruptions
20. Vast right-wing conspiracy
21. Russian reset button
22. Benghazi: Spontaneous protest triggered by anti-Muslim video
23. J. Christopher Stevens
24. Sean Smith
25. Tyrone S. Woods
26. Glen Doherty
27. "Why aren't I fifty points ahead?"
28. "Ruff, ruff, ruff!"
29. "Basket of deplorables"
30. "Racist"
31. "Sexist"
32. "Homophobic"
33. "Xenophobic"
34. "Islamaphobic"
35. "Irredeemable"
36. "Not America"
37. Above the law
38. Private Server
39. BleachBit
40. Clinton Foundation

41. Michelle Obama

42. "For the first time in my adult life, I'm proud of my country." (2008)

43. Nanny state school lunch program

44. "See, now, we are feeling what not having hope feels like." (Dec. 2016)

45. Vladimir Putin
... NOT!

46. Joe Biden

47. "This is a big ___ing deal."

48. Tim Kaine

49. Bernie Sanders*

50. Harry Reid*

51. Nancy Pelosi*

52. "We have to pass the bill so you can find out what is in it."

53. Mitt Romney

54. John McCain

55. Jeb Bush

56. Lindsey Graham

57. Assoc. Justice
Elena Kagen

58. Assoc. Justice Sonia Sotomayer

59. Assoc. Justice Stephen G. Breyer

60. Assoc. Justice
Ruth Bader Ginsberg

61. Chief Justice John G. Roberts, Jr.

62. Death of Assoc. Justice Antonin Scalia

63. Valerie Jarrett

64. Susan Rice on
the Sunday shows

65. Donna Brazile

66. Huma Abedin

67. Judicial activism

68. Congress

69. RINOs

70. Wimpy
conservatives

71. D. C. Swamp …
Government waste and
corruption

72. Hyper-partisanship

73. Obstructionism

74. Radical Islamic Terrorism

75. San Bernardino
Christmas party

76. Orlando Pulse Night Club

77. Fort Hood
"workplace violence"

78. Boston Marathon/Boston Strong

79. Terror attacks in Paris, Nice and Brussels

80. Terrorists released from Guantanamo Bay … recidivism

81. TSA patting down granny

82. Veterans dying while waiting for VA care

83.   WikiLeaks

84.   Julian Assange

85.   Edward Snowden

86.   Political correctness run amok

87.   Identity politics

88. Transgender bathrooms

89. Christian cake makers and wedding photographers being run out of business

90. Constant use of the race card

91. Constant comparisons to Nazis

92.   Constant claims of a war on women

93. NOW

94. Women's movements that exclude 50% of women and ignore the plight of human rights violations against women in other countries, especially under Sharia Law

95.   Choice only applies to abortion but not schools, healthcare or any other aspect of life

96. Planned Parenthood … or Baby Body Parts R Us

97. "Free" college tuition

98. "Free" everything

99. Social Security going broke

100. Entitlement expansion, waste and fraud

101. Depleted
military/Sequester

102. Devastating losses of blood and treasure without victory

103. Politicization of Federal bureaucracies

104. IRS Scandal

105. John Koskinen

106. Lois Lerner

107. Obama Administration's surveillance of James Rosen

108. Wussification of America

109. Snowflakes

110. Campus Safe Zones

111. Attacks on the 1st Amendment

112. Indictment of Dinesh D'Souza

113. Attacks on the 2nd Amendment

114. Eric Holder

115. Fast and Furious Scandal

116. Intolerance of the "tolerant" Left

117. Bloated Big Government

118. Pensions failing

119. Stagnant wages

120. Proliferation of part-time work … (30-hour limit)

121.   Tight credit for small businesses

122. Health insurance but virtually no healthcare … high premiums and high deductibles

123. Jonathan Gruber

124. "Lack of transparency is a huge political advantage … stupidity of the American voter"

125. Bill Clinton

126. Obamacare: "the craziest thing in the world"

127. Government
mandates and penalties

128. Highest corporate taxes in the industrialized world

129. High individual
   income tax rates and
   plethora of other taxes
   … real estate,
   property, sales, etc.

130. Highly complicated tax code and burdensome returns

131. Capital and jobs fleeing to foreign countries

132. Oversaturation from the relentless, 24/7 news cycle

133. Decay of
journalistic standards

134. Untrustworthy media

135. Unreliable polling

136. Fake news

137. ABC

138. CBS

139. NBC

140. CNN

141. MSNBC

142. NPR

143. Huffington Post

144. Mother Jones

145. New York Times

146. Washington Post

147. Rolling Stone

148. Daily Kos

149. Chris Matthews

150. Matt Lauer

151. Joy Behar

152. Whoopi Goldberg

153. Candy Crowley

154. Jake Tapper

155. Juan Williams

156. Jon Stewart

157. Van Jones

158. Stephen Colbert

159. Maureen Dowd

160. Major Garrett

161. Joe Scarborough

162. Christopher Hitchens

163. Bill Moyers

164. Rachael Maddow

165. Paul Krugman

166. Geraldo Rivera

167. Leslie Marshall

168. Shepherd Smith

169. Megan Kelly

170. Richard Fowler

171. Jehmu Green

172. Jorge Ramos

173. Scott Pelley

174. Hollywood Propaganda Machine

175. Oprah Winfrey

176. George Clooney

177. Madonna

178. Ashley Judd

179. Robert De Niro

180. Rosie O'Donnell

181. Chelsea Handler

182. Cher

183. Katie Perry

184. Michael Moore

185. SNL

186. Failing public schools

187. Political indoctrination in schools and universities

188. NEA and AFT

189. AARP

190. Anarchists posing as protesters

191. Occupy Wall Street

192. George Soros

193. Black Lives Matter

194. "Pigs in a blanket"

195. War on police

196. "What do we want? Dead Cops!"

197. Grievance Industry

198. Al Sharpton

199. Ferguson, Missouri

200. Jay Nixon (Nero fiddled while Ferguson burned)

201. Hands Up, Don't Shoot

202. Baltimore, Maryland

203. Marilyn Mosby

204. Heroin epidemic

205. Sex trafficking

206. Ten Commandments removed from courtrooms

207. Prayer prohibited at high school football games

208. Bibles banned in public schools while the Koran is used for "cultural purposes"

209. Parents rights diminished in favor of a "village"

210. Stifling, business-killing regulations

211. Sarbanes-Oxley

212. Dodd Frank

213. DOL Fiduciary Rule

214. EPA

215. Farmers being put out of business to save endangered insects

216. Animas River in Colorado poisoned by EPA

217. Puddle on your land gives the EPA the right to manage it as a protected wetland

218. Keystone Pipeline

219. Dakota Access Pipeline

220. Militarized U. S. Bureau of Land Management versus Cliven Bundy

221. Enviromaniacs

222. Al Gore

223. Climate Change hysteria

224. Carbon Credits

225. NOAA's climate change hoax prior to 2015 U. N. Summit in Paris

226. "Settled Science"/Thought Coercion

227. Rigged computer climate models

228. Falsified climate data

229. Crumbling U. S. Infrastructure after waste of $800 billion stimulus

230. Decaying inner cities after 50 years of Progressive rule

231. Skyrocketing murder rates in major cities like Chicago

232. Crony Capitalism

233. Globalism

234. America portrayed as the villain

235. Open borders

236. Kate Steinle

237. Detective Michael Davis

238. Deputy Sheriff Danny Oliver

239. Jamiel Shaw, Jr.

240. Failed foreign
   policy that emboldens
   enemies while
   undermining allies

241. Loss of American prestige around the world

242. Ineffective vetting of immigrants and refugees

243. Chinese expansion
in South China Sea

244. Russian Imperialism

245. Iranian provocations

246. North Korean Provocations

247. Special rights versus equal rights

248. Sen. Mark Begich, AK*

249. Sen. Blanche Lincoln, AR*

250. Sen. Mark Pryor, AR*

251. Sen. Barbara Boxer, CA*

252. Sen. Dianne Feinstein, CA*

253. Sen. Michael Bennett, CO*

254. Sen. Mark Udall, CO*

255. Sen. Christopher Dodd, CT*

256. Sen. Joe Lieberman, CT*

257. Sen. Thomas Carper, DE*

258. Sen. Edward Kaufman, DE*

259. Sen. Bill Nelson, FL*

260. Sen. Daniel Akaka, HI*

261. Sen. Daniel Inouye, HI*

262. Sen. Thomas Harkin, IA*

263. Sen. Roland Burris, IL*

264. Sen. Richard
    Durbin, IL*
265. Sen. Evan Bayh,
    IN*
266. Sen. Mary
    Landrieu, LA*
267. Sen. John Kerry,
    MA*
268. Sen. Paul Kirk,
    MA*
269. Sen. Benjamin
    Cardin, MD*
270. Sen. Barbara
    Mikulski, MD*
271. Sen. Carl Levin,
    MI*

272. Sen. Debbie
Stabenow, MI*

273. Sen. Alan Franken,
MN*

274. Sen. Amy
Klobuchar, MN*

275. Sen. Claire
McCaskill, MO*

276. Sen. Max Baucus,
MT*

277. Sen. Jon Tester,
MT*

278. Sen. Kay Hagan,
NC*

279. Sen. Kent Conrad,
ND*

280. Sen. Byron Dorgan, ND*

281. Sen. Ben Nelson, NE*

282. Sen. Jeanne Shaheen, NH*

283. Sen. Frank Lautenberg, NJ*

284. Sen. Robert Menendez, NJ*

285. Sen. Jeff Bingaman, NM*

286. Sen. Tom Udall, NM*

287. Sen. Kirsten Gillibrand, NY*

288. Sen. Charles Schumer, NY*

289. Sen. Sherrod Brown, OH*

290. Sen. Jeff Merkley, OR*

291. Sen. Ron Wyden, OR*

292. Sen. Robert Casey, PA*

293. Sen. Arlen Specter, PA*

294. Sen. John Reed, RI*

295. Sen. Sheldon Whitehouse, RI*

296. Sen. Tim Johnson, SD*

297. Sen. Mark Warner, VA*

298. Sen. Jim Webb, VA*

299. Sen. Patrick Leahy, VT*

300. Sen. Maria Cantwell, WA*

301. Sen. Patty Murray, WA*

302. Sen. Russell Feingold, WI*

303. Sen. Herbert Kohl, WI*

304. Sen. Robert Byrd, WV*

305. Sen. John
    Rockefeller, WV*
306. Sen. Jim Bunning,
    KY**
307. Rep. Ann
    Kirkpatrick, AZ*
308. Rep. Ed Pastor,
    AZ*
309. Rep. Harry
    Mitchell, AZ*
310. Rep. Raul Grijalva,
    AZ*
311. Rep. Gabrielle
    Giffords, AZ*
312. Rep. Vic Snyder,
    AR*

313. Rep. Mike Thompson, CA*
314. Rep. Doris Matsui, CA*
315. Rep. Lynn Woolsey, CA*
316. Rep. George Miller, CA*
317. Rep. Barbara Lee, CA*
318. Rep. John Garamendi, CA*
319. Rep. Jerry McNerney, CA*
320. Rep. Jackie Speier, CA*

321. Rep. Pete Stark, CA*

322. Rep. Anna Eshoo, CA*

323. Rep. Mike Honda, CA*

324. Rep. Zoe Lofgren, CA*

325. Rep. Sam Farr, CA*

326. Rep. Dennis Cardoza, CA*

327. Rep. Jim Costa, CA*

328. Rep. Lois Capps, CA*

329. Rep. Brad Sherman, CA*

330. Rep. Howard
Berman, CA*

331. Rep. Adam Schiff,
CA*

332. Rep. Henry
Waxman, CA*

333. Rep. Xavier
Becerra, CA*

334. Rep. Judy Chu,
CA*

335. Rep. Diane Watson,
CA*

336. Rep. Lucille
Roybal-Allard, CA*

337. Rep. Maxine
Waters, CA*

338. Rep. Jane Harman, CA*

339. Rep. Laura Richardson, CA*

340. Rep. Grace Napolitano, CA*

341. Rep. Linda Sanchez, CA*

342. Rep. Joe Baca, CA*

343. Rep. Loretta Sanchez, CA*

344. Rep. Bob Filner, CA*

345. Rep. Susan Davis, CA*

346. Rep. Diana DeGette, CO*

347. Rep. Jared Polis, CO*

348. Rep. John Salazar, CO*

349. Rep. Betsy Markey, CO*

350. Rep. Ed Perlmutter, CO*

351. Rep. John Larson, CT*

352. Rep. Joe Courtney, CT*

353. Rep. Rosa DeLauro, CT*

354. Rep. James Himes, CT*

355. Rep. Christopher Murphy, CT*

356. Rep. Allen Boyd, FL*

357. Rep. Corinne Brown, FL*

358. Rep. Alan Grayson, FL*

359. Rep. Kathy Castor, FL*

360. Rep. Kendrick Meek, FL*

361. Rep. Debbie Wasserman Schultz, FL*

362. Rep. Ron Klein, FL*

363. Rep. Alcee
    Hastings, FL*
364. Rep. Suzanne
    Kosmas, FL*
365. Rep. Sanford
    Bishop, GA*
366. Rep. Hank Johnson,
    GA*
367. Rep. John Lewis,
    GA*
368. Rep. David Scott,
    GA*
369. Rep. Mazie Hirono,
    HI*
370. Rep. Bobby Rush,
    IL*

371. Rep. Jesse Jackson, IL*

372. Rep. Luis Gutierrez, IL*

373. Rep. Mike Quigley, IL*

374. Rep. Danny Davis, IL*

375. Rep. Melissa Bean, IL*

376. Rep. Jan Schakowsky, IL*

377. Rep. Deborah Halvorson, IL*

378. Rep. Jerry Costello, IL*

379. Rep. Bill Foster, IL*

380. Rep. Phil Hare, IL*

381. Rep. Peter Visclosky, IN*

382. Rep. Joe Donnelly, IN*

383. Rep. Andre Carson, IN*

384. Rep. Brad Ellsworth, IN*

385. Rep. Baron Hill, IN*

386. Rep. Bruce Braley, IA*

387. Rep. David Loebsack, IA*

388. Rep. Leonard Boswell, IA*

389. Rep. Dennis Moore, KS*

390. Rep. John Yarmuth, KY*

391. Rep. Chellie Pingree, ME*

392. Rep. Mike Michaud, ME*

393. Rep. A. Dutch Ruppersberger, MD*

394. Rep. John Sarbanes, MD*

395. Rep. Donna Edwards, MD*

396. Rep. Steny Hoyer, MD*

397. Rep. Elijah Cummings, MD*

398. Rep. Chris Van Hollen, MD*

399. Rep. John Olver, MA*

400. Rep. Richard Neal, MA*

401. Rep. Jim McGovern, MA*

402. Rep. Barney Frank, MA*

403. Rep. Niki Tsongas, MA*

404. Rep. John Tierney, MA*

405. Rep. Ed Markey, MA*

406. Rep. Michael Capuano, MA*

407. Rep. Bill Delahunt, MA*

408. Rep. Bart Stupak, MI*

409. Rep. Dale Kildee, MI*

410. Rep. Mark Schauer, MI*

411. Rep. Gary Peters, MI*

412. Rep. Sander Levin, MI*

413. Rep. Carolyn Kilpatrick, MI*

414. Rep. John Conyers, MI*

415. Rep. John Dingell, MI*

416. Rep. Timothy Walz, MN*

417. Rep. Betty McCollum, MN*

418. Rep. Keith Ellison, MN*

419. Rep. James Oberstar, MN*

420. Rep. Bennie
     Thompson, MS*
421. Rep. Lacy Clay,
     MO*
422. Rep. Russ
     Carnahan, MO*
423. Rep. Emanuel
     Cleaver, MO*
424. Rep. Shelley
     Berkley, NV*
425. Rep. Dina Titus,
     NV*
426. Rep. Carol Shea-
     Porter, NH*
427. Rep. Paul Hodes,
     NH*

428. Rep. Rob Andrews, NJ*

429. Rep. Frank Pallone, NJ*

430. Rep. Bill Pascrell, NJ*

431. Rep. Steven Rothman, NJ*

432. Rep. Donald Payne, NJ*

433. Rep. Rush Holt, NJ*

434. Rep. Albio Sires, NJ*

435. Rep. Martin Heinrich, NM*

436. Rep. Ben Lujan, NM*

437. Rep. Timothy Bishop, NY*

438. Rep. Steve Israel, NY*

439. Rep. Carolyn McCarthy, NY*

440. Rep. Gary Ackerman, NY*

441. Rep. Gregory Meeks, NY*

442. Rep. Joe Crowley, NY*

443. Rep. Jerrold Nadler, NY*

444. Rep. Anthony Wiener, NY*

445. Rep. Ed Towns, NY*

446. Rep. Yvette Clarke, NY*

447. Rep. Nydia Velazquez, NY*

448. Rep. Carolyn Maloney, NY*

449. Rep. Charles Rangel, NY*

450. Rep. Jose Serrano, NY*

451. Rep. Eliot Engel, NY*

452. Rep. Nita Lowey, NY*

453. Rep. John Hall, NY*

454. Rep. Scott Murphy, NY*

455. Rep. Paul Tonko, NY*

456. Rep. Maurice Hinchey, NY*

457. Rep. William Owens, NY*

458. Rep. Daniel Maffei, NY*

459. Rep. Brian Higgins, NY*

460. Rep. Louise
   Slaughter, NY*
461. Rep. G. K.
   Butterfield, NC*
462. Rep. Bob Etheridge,
   NC*
463. Rep. David Price,
   NC*
464. Rep. Mel Watt,
   NC*
465. Rep. Brad Miller,
   NC*
466. Rep. Earl Pomeroy,
   ND*
467. Rep. Steve
   Driehaus, OH*

468. Rep. Charles
Wilson, OH*

469. Rep. Marcy Kaptur,
OH*

470. Rep. Dennis
Kucinich, OH*

471. Rep. Marcia Fudge,
OH*

472. Rep. Betty Sutton,
OH*

473. Rep. Mary Jo
Kilroy, OH*

474. Rep. John Boccieri,
OH*

475. Rep. Tim Ryan,
OH*

476. Rep. David Wu,
OR*

477. Rep. Earl
Blumenauer, OR*

478. Rep. Peter DeFazio,
OR*

479. Rep. Kurt Schrader,
OR*

480. Rep. Robert Brady,
PA*

481. Rep. Chaka Fattah,
PA*

482. Rep. Kathleen
Dahlkemper, PA*

483. Rep. Joe Sestak,
PA*

484. Rep. Patrick
Murphy, PA*

485. Rep. Christopher
Carney, PA*

486. Rep. Paul
Kanjorski, PA*

487. Rep. Allyson
Schwartz, PA*

488. Rep. Mike Doyle,
PA*

489. Rep. Patrick
Kennedy, RI*

490. Rep. Jim Langevin,
RI*

491. Rep. John Spratt,
SC*

492. Rep. Jim Clyburn, SC*

493. Rep. Jim Cooper, TN*

494. Rep. Bart Gordon, TN*

495. Rep. Steve Cohen, TN*

496. Rep. Al Green, TX*

497. Rep. Ruben Hinojosa, TX*

498. Rep. Silvestre Reyes, TX*

499. Rep. Sheila Jackson Lee, TX*

500. Rep. Charles Gonzalez, TX*

501. Rep. Ciro
    Rodriguez, TX*
502. Rep. Lloyd
    Doggett, TX*
503. Rep. Solomon
    Ortiz, TX*
504. Rep. Henry Cuellar,
    TX*
505. Rep. Gene Green,
    TX*
506. Rep. Eddie
    Johnson, TX*
507. Rep. Peter Welch,
    VT*
508. Rep. Bobby Scott,
    VA*

509. Rep. Thomas Perriello, VA*

510. Rep. Jim Moran, VA*

511. Rep. Gerald Connolly, VA*

512. Rep. Jay Inslee, WA*

513. Rep. Rick Larsen, WA*

514. Rep. Brian Baird, WA*

515. Rep. Norm Dicks, WA*

516. Rep. Jim McDermott, WA*

517. Rep. Adam Smith, WA*

518. Rep. Alan Mollohan, WV*

519. Rep. Nick Rahall, WV*

520. Rep. Tammy Baldwin, WI*

521. Rep. Ron Kind, WI*

522. Rep. Gwen Moore, WI*

523. Rep. Dave Obey, WI*

524. Rep. Steve Kagen, WI*

525. Eroding freedoms

526. Lost liberty

527. Undermining of the Constitution

528. The Trump Family

529.
Donald J.
Trump

530.
God/Jesus Christ

(*) Voted in favor of the Affordable Care Act/Obamacare

(**) Sen. Bunning did not vote on the Affordable Care Act/Obamacare. He was the only Republican Senator that did not vote against ACA.

The final vote tallies in Congress were as follows.

House: Democrats 219 yes & 34 no

Republicans 0 yes & 178 no

Senate: Democrats 60 yes & 0 no

Republicans 0 yes & 39 no with Senator

Bunning of KY not voting.

BIBLIOGRAPHY

Everything in this book is based on information in the public domain. Thus, I have no references to cite. The opinions offered herein reflect my independent news consumption and personal analysis of current events through the internet and various news outlets. I'd like to offer my appreciation to some of my favorite journalists and commentators who, in my opinion, provide fair, objective and honest coverage … in no particular order.

Steve Doocy, Ainsley Earhardt, Brian Kilmeade, Jamie Allman, Marc Cox, Laura Ingraham, Bill Hemmer, Martha McCallum, Jon Scott, Jenna Lee, Neil Cavuto, Rush Limbaugh, Dana Loesch, Charles Payne, Charles Krauthammer, Mark Levin, Herman Cain, Sheriff David Clarke, Col. Allen West, Gen. Jack Keane, Bret Baier, Tucker Carlson, Sean Hannity, Maria Bartiromo, Newt Gingrich, Chris Stirewalt, Greg Gutfeld, Kimberly Guilfoyle, Pete Hegseth, Brit Hume, Harris Faulkner, Katie Pavlich, Walid Phares, John Roberts, Andrew Napolitano, Oliver North, Chris Matthews, Stuart Varney, Abby Huntsman, Doug Schoen, Jesse Watters, Jeanine Pirro and Shannon Bream … and my apologies to all the other great ones I've failed to mention.

Please note that I do not know any of these people personally and do not mean to imply that they in any way endorse this book or the opinions contained herein.

Final Thoughts:

Pick any name or event listed herein and one could ascribe a positive or negative impact on the election of 2016 depending upon one's political leanings. For example, it would be easy to make the case that someone like Megan Kelly, intentionally or unintentionally, influenced some people to support Donald Trump while simultaneously causing others to back Hillary Clinton. However, few would argue that she didn't have some effect on the outcome. When viewed as a whole though, I believe the list in its entirety tipped the scales in Donald Trump's favor.

Based on Reason #530, do I believe that God had a hand in this election? Yes, I am convinced in this sense. I do not know if Donald Trump is a Christian. For his sake and ours, I hope so but it's not for me to say since I can't see into his heart and can only make assumptions based on the fruit he bears and his own testimony. However, it doesn't matter in that God has used believers and non-believers throughout history to accomplish His good purposes. Regarding the latter, take for example pagan King Cyrus who ruled Persia from 539-530 B. C. God used him as His instrument in freeing the Israelites from 70 years of Babylonian captivity, returning them to their homeland and rebuilding the Temple. This fulfilled God's incredibly specific prophesy that Isaiah proclaimed 150 years in advance.

Donald Trump was not my first, second or third choice but he eventually won me over. From hindsight, I can see how God's wisdom is infinitely greater than mine. Donald Trump possesses an incredible, seemingly inexhaustible store of energy and resolve that makes him perfectly suited to tackle the monumental difficulties facing our nation. Any other politician would have wilted under the intense pressure he has faced from an opposition hell-bent on stopping him at any cost. So yes, I believe God has equipped Donald Trump to serve Him and our nation at this particular point in our history. May God bless President Trump, all of us Deplorables, all of our people … and may God continue to bless the United States of America.

Other Books by Steve Stranghoener:

Deadly Preference (coming soon)

Veeper

Ferguson Miracle

God-Whacked!

Cha-Cha Chandler: Teen Demonologist

Straight Talk about Christian Misconceptions

The Last Prophet: Doomsday Diary

The Last Prophet: Imminent End

Murder by Chance: Blood Moon Lunacy of
Lew Carew

Asunder: The Tale of the Renaissance Killer

Tracts in Time

All of these titles are available under
Books/Steve Stranghoener at
www.amazon.com.

www.ingramcontent.com/pod-product-compliance
Lightning Source LLC
Chambersburg PA
CBHW062133280526
45788CB00001B/151